T0132357

CHARLES MORRISON

Announcing
GOD'S
GOVERNMENT

Poetic Expressions of Faith

Announcing GOD'S GOVERNMENT
POETIC EXPRESSIONS OF FAITH

iUniverse books may be ordered through booksellers or by contacting:

iUniverse
1663 Liberty Drive
Bloomington, IN 47403
www.iuniverse.com
1-800-Authors (1-800-288-4677)

Because of the dynamic nature of the Internet, any web addresses or links contained in this book may have changed since publication and may no longer be valid. The views expressed in this work are solely those of the author and do not necessarily reflect the views of the publisher, and the publisher hereby disclaims any responsibility for them.

Any people depicted in stock imagery provided by Getty Images are models, and such images are being used for illustrative purposes only. Certain stock imagery © Getty Images.

ISBN: 978-1-5320-3672-9 (sc)
ISBN: 978-1-5320-3673-6 (e)

Library of Congress Control Number: 2017917205

Print information available on the last page.

iUniverse rev. date: 05/08/2018

WWW.ANNOUNCINGGODSGOVERNMENT.COM

INDARKNESSGLOW@GMAIL.COM

Crazy times in the world, as we face division in government, race and religion, as we scurry about daily trying to make a living for our families, by means of an oppressive system, a system that ravages like a beast, a system that promotes drugs, immorality, violence and materialism. A system that uses mainstream media, commercialism and entertainment to turn truth into false, to disguise bad as good, and to reduce importance into insignificance. Truly dark times!

Announcing God's Government, Poetic Expressions of Faith is a collection of poems written over a span of time. Inspired by faith in God, His future promises for the Heavens, the Earth and Mankind. It also includes poetry influenced by life experiences. It has and continues to be a journey, highs and lows, accomplishment and failure, growth and regress.

As a company, it is Moon Daddy's ultimate goal to illuminate light in dark times and to glow in a dark place.

The Author

THE CAUSE

"As we sit calm watching the sitcom, we're being programmed by the program."
Charles Morrison

TO CONTROL
THE MIND

IS TO CONTROL
BODY

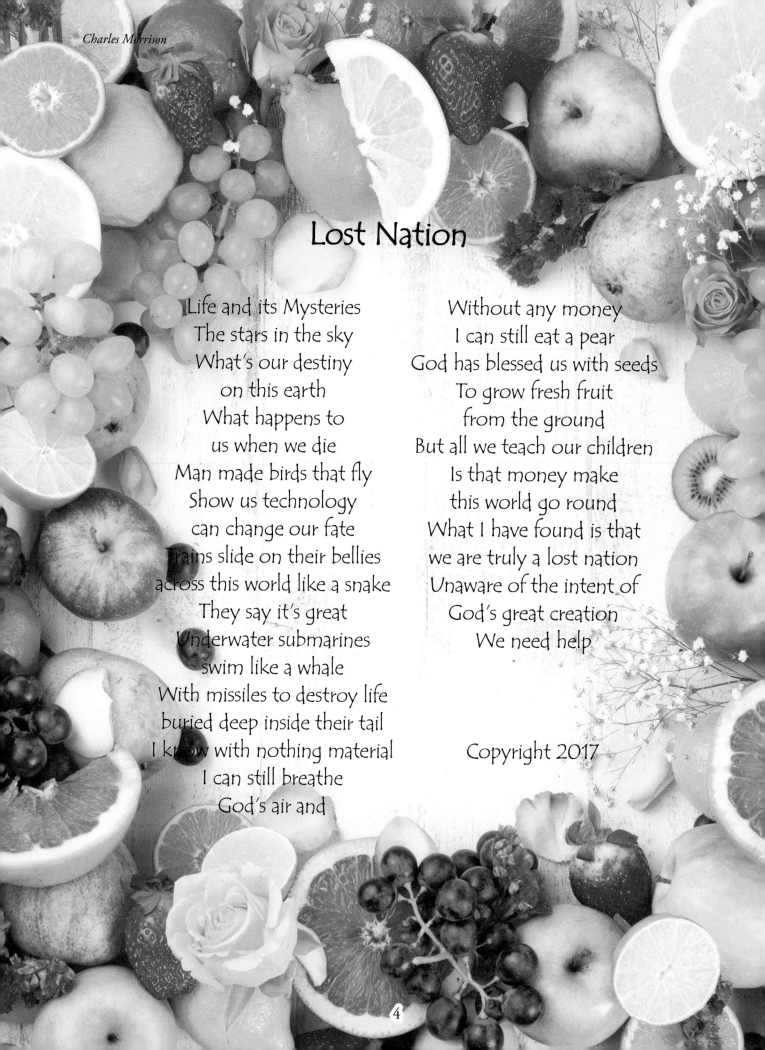

Charles Morrison

Lost Nation

Life and its Mysteries
The stars in the sky
What's our destiny
on this earth
What happens to
us when we die
Man made birds that fly
Show us technology
can change our fate
Trains slide on their bellies
across this world like a snake
They say it's great
Underwater submarines
swim like a whale
With missiles to destroy life
buried deep inside their tail
I know with nothing material
I can still breathe
God's air and

Without any money
I can still eat a pear
God has blessed us with seeds
To grow fresh fruit
from the ground
But all we teach our children
Is that money make
this world go round
What I have found is that
we are truly a lost nation
Unaware of the intent of
God's great creation
We need help

Copyright 2017

Slave Mentality

From our natural state in nature
We were taken on economy behalf
From our natural state of mind we have been separated from
Today we are blind
Over time we have found comfort
We have become dependant on this man
In our natural environment
Our necessities was provided by land
They have turned my brother against me with distrust
Now it's a must I watch his hand
Being separated from my wife
She's being taught a new way of life
So she will now teach my seed
That obedience to the master will satisfy their need
Then they will teach their seed
To obey the voice of their owner
From generation to generation
This cycle grows stronger and stronger
Today on its own axial this cycle revolve
But with faith in the true God
Backed up by works
It can be solved

Copyright 2017

Where's the Love

Everything is business
It's never personal
Where the love go
We have no time for love
Because we all chasing dough
Every morning we wake up
We off to our business
Whether it's school, the doctor, work, or false religion
It's all we teach our children
Our children not taught Gods truth
So they can really benefit their self
They're taught business, technology, war and worldly wealth
We need to open our eyes wider
Look a little deeper
The truth is in our face
But we too busy on our cell phones
And our ears plugged up with speakers
Just peep us
The truth hurts
Deceit is so deceiving
But in prayer with sincere ness and repentance
Then we can receive Him
The only true God

Copyright 2017

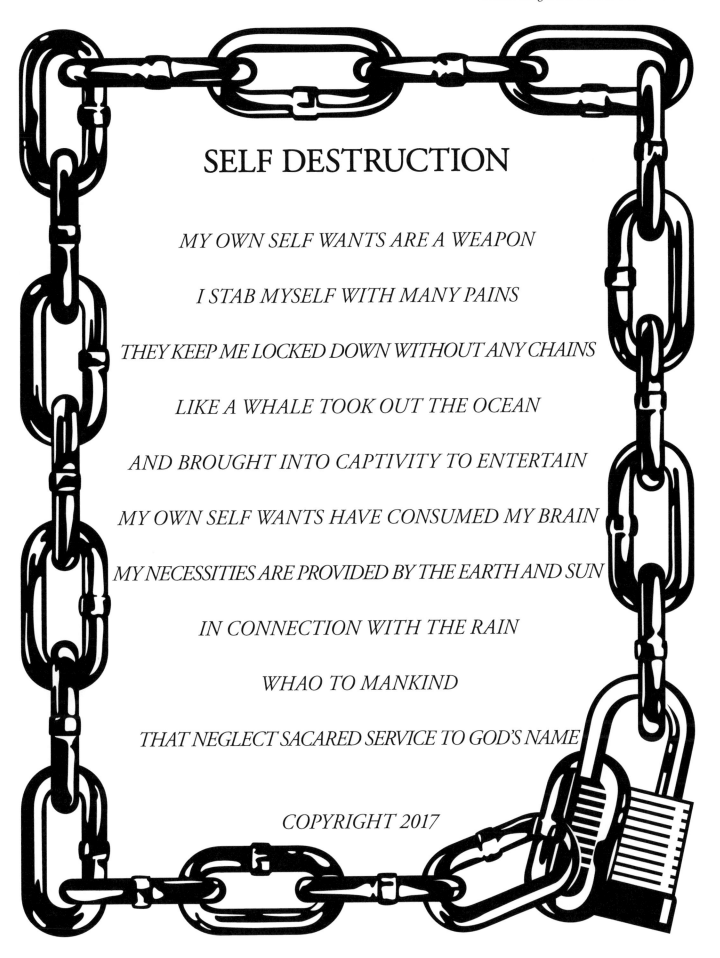

SELF DESTRUCTION

MY OWN SELF WANTS ARE A WEAPON

I STAB MYSELF WITH MANY PAINS

THEY KEEP ME LOCKED DOWN WITHOUT ANY CHAINS

LIKE A WHALE TOOK OUT THE OCEAN

AND BROUGHT INTO CAPTIVITY TO ENTERTAIN

MY OWN SELF WANTS HAVE CONSUMED MY BRAIN

MY NECESSITIES ARE PROVIDED BY THE EARTH AND SUN

IN CONNECTION WITH THE RAIN

WHAO TO MANKIND

THAT NEGLECT SACARED SERVICE TO GOD'S NAME

COPYRIGHT 2017

UNTITLED

The devil always gone flee from the word of the truth
Temptation is all he has
Burger stands on every corner
Women that's loose
Money, power, wealth
We are all our own gods
We all serve our self
From the beginning we were tricked
Taken from our natural state
The moment we took our own path
And from the fruit we ate
Every since then it's been
Business, immorality, and hate
We can not forget about the drugs
It's not even a debate
We have to open our eyes
Look past the surface
This world is the worst
No man made government on this earth can work it
Or fix it
I try not to mix in it
Exist in it
I try to stay loyal
A true witness
The spirit of this world
I have to keep resisting it

Copyright2017

My Life Partner

My woman my wife my companion and partner in life
What will she be like
Perhaps the beauty of Sarah
I becoming lost in her eyes in which I would stare
Or maybe the earnestness of Hannah persevering in prayer
A woman strong in faith
Reflecting Gods glory a quality that's rare
Not in competition not catty
Not envious or jealous
But in Gods arrangement is where she would relish
As a daughter in law of Noah
Escaping Gods judgment
The secret place of her heart
Being her adornment
Having deep respect for her husband
Knowing this has great value in Gods eyes
And never ignoring it
In example after Abigail, Anna, Deborah and Ruth
Courageous, submissive, patient, sensible
Loving Gods truth
Having the good portion like Mary
But taking care of home like Martha too
Bellowing out praise and thanks to God
Never ceasing to give God her best
As I pray thanking Him for this woman
That is bone of my bone and flesh of my flesh

Copyright2017

Emotions

Do I control my emotions or;
Do my emotions control me
Do I have a short fuse or;
Do I have a long wick
When my patience run thin
I emotionally react quick
It's a fact emotions make me speak hate
When I really love
Hate turns into rage
Inwardly emotions got me burning up
I have to stand strong when the heat is on
Emotions cause a blur
I can't tell the difference between right and wrong
But I'm the king that's on the throne
The one that's in command
My emotions are submissive to me
They react on my demand
I send them to their rightful position
In the pit of my stomach
Deep inside my soul
The battle is won
But the war continues
For now I'm the one in control

Copyright 2017

Decisions

One man
One million decisions
Should I or;
Shouldn't I
Modern day riches
Or eternal life
Fornication and lust
Or love and my wife
Destroy my body with drugs and wine
Or glorify my body with Gods spirit
That's divine
Should I or;
Shouldn't I
Live for today or;
Live for tomorrow
One man
One million decisions

COPYRIGHT 2017

Road of Life

I have witnessed road rage
Went the wrong way down one-ways
For days and months I have been lost
It's like I been in a maze
So many ways
So many other roads
Yeah, I could have went
But I'm addicted to the flash
Plus the cash is what pays the rent
A Harvard education couldn't touch the corners I have bent
Head on collisions
Quick decisions
I have ran some red lights
Most people would be dead or in jail
If they were stuck in my life
I have paid the price
I've crashed time after time
Trying to speed down this road
I've paid fine after fine
There have been a few casualties
And the fault was all mines
With time I come to realize
Traveling this road is not a race
It's just an end to a means
To help you to reach a certain place
The moral to the story is
Be careful what you chase
The best things in life are free
And they are right before our face

Copyright2017

The Rebirth

The world through my eyes
Is in chaos and full of sin
Every door that I open
Every room that I walk in
All the people that I talk to
All their conversation has been
Is about girls and money
Cars and cloths
They get mad at me
Cause I'm talking about saving my soul
I'm talking about having control
I'm talking about spiritual growth
That's why I'm transformed
I Release, I restore, I recover and I'm reborn
Like a caterpillar in a cocoon
Like a baby in its mother womb
I'm not fully developed yet
But my spiritual birth is coming soon

Copyright 2017

THE EFFECT

"Do I suffer because I'm an artist, or am I an artist because I suffer?"
Thomas Kinkade
(Painter of Light)

DYSFUNCTION HAS BECOME THE NEW NORMAL

One or the Other

This whole entertainment industry
Is watered down
Everyone is giving praises to idol gods
With their own style
It's foul
It's time to truly do some soul searching
The reality of it all
It's our own self who we really hurting
Instead of blurting out what we have materially
And promoting lewd sex
What's up with reaching in
And lifting each other spiritually
To what is next
We need to make Gods Kingdom our future
Learn from mistakes of our history
Put all faith in God
He will unlock all the mysteries
Mention He
And the wicked one will flee instantly
It's plain to see
You either serve God
Or you serve the devil
There is no in between

Copyright 2017

The Word of God

Wars and rumors of wars
Earthquakes, floods and wildfires
Diseases like AIDS, Cancer
and the West Nile virus
The time is upon us
It's a must that we put
trust in the True God
Not in materialism and commercialism
In which the devil hide
Yes this is a crying time
But let not our hearts be troubled
But let our awareness be strengthen
The Word of God
The only thing that can get our minds
Back to their rightful position
In addition it promise us eternal life
The Word of God
The only food in which we eat
And it sheds light
Brightness, guidance from the dark
In prayer with repentance and
Sincerity is where it starts

Copyright2017

Just as the Days of Noah

The world scene I seen
I mean I saw
I see it now
Times worst than Noah's day
No one taking notice
The spirit of the air is all around
Our values revolve around the value of the dollar
They say it make the world go round
But what I have really found
Is quickly it bring us down
Inhabitants of the earth
Living souls that walk the ground
It wasn't meant for man to direct his own step
A flood destroyed all life only eight souls where left
What does that tell you
About the inclination of a mans heart
It gets deep
Rewind back to the start
After mass clouds were created and
There was separation between light and dark
It was us man
As then as today
We fall victim to our own plan

Copyright 2017

Man Made Gold

No matter who we are, we're stuck
No matter where we are, we're stuck
No matter what we do, we're stuck
We all have that in common
We're all shackled by the same link chain
Our daily living, our bills, our expenses
Economics
Everywhere we go
There's always someone waiting for that dough
That bread, it has the whole scared
Can't picture life without
It provide food for our mouth
It keeps us sheltered in a house
It gets us everything
Heat, lights, water
Hair and health care
As long as we have it
There's nothing else we care about
Copper, silver, gold
Paper, plastic, credit
Many forms, but all the same
Soon to be a change
Whether it is change in our pockets
Or our accounts have billions of dollars
Whether we are uneducated or a scholar
No matter if we are a slave or if we're free
Soon society will see
That we all have inherited the culture of the beast
Economics
Our daily living, our bills, our expenses
We're all shacked by the same link chain
We all have that in common
No matter what we do, we're stuck
No matter where we are, we're stuck
No matter who we are, we're stuck
That man made gold
That almighty dollar

Copyright 2017

Charles Morrison

Out to Conquer

I'm out to conquer the world
What am I really up against
Spirit creatures preserved in tartarus
No place in Gods memory for them
Dense darkness is where they exist
Family opposition no love
Being left alone
Knowing that bad association
Leads to works that's wrong
The desire of my flesh
That's in contrast with my mind
I'm up against
Living for my own self
Becoming a blind guide
But it's in Jehovah's strength I must reside
He's the one that's on my side
His holy spirit He provide
His word the Bible He gives as light
In order to conquer the world
In His law I must take delight
Night and day I must read and pray
Walking with Him daily
Never becoming a sheep that stray
In order to conquer the world
I must follow Gods son
Jesus Christ example
He is the one that leads the way

LOST TIME

Where has time gone

For it was just here

What seems like yesterday

Has been a few years

As I stare in this mirror

I wonder

Who is this aged man

Reflecting back on memories

Wishing I had it all to do again

Copyright 2017

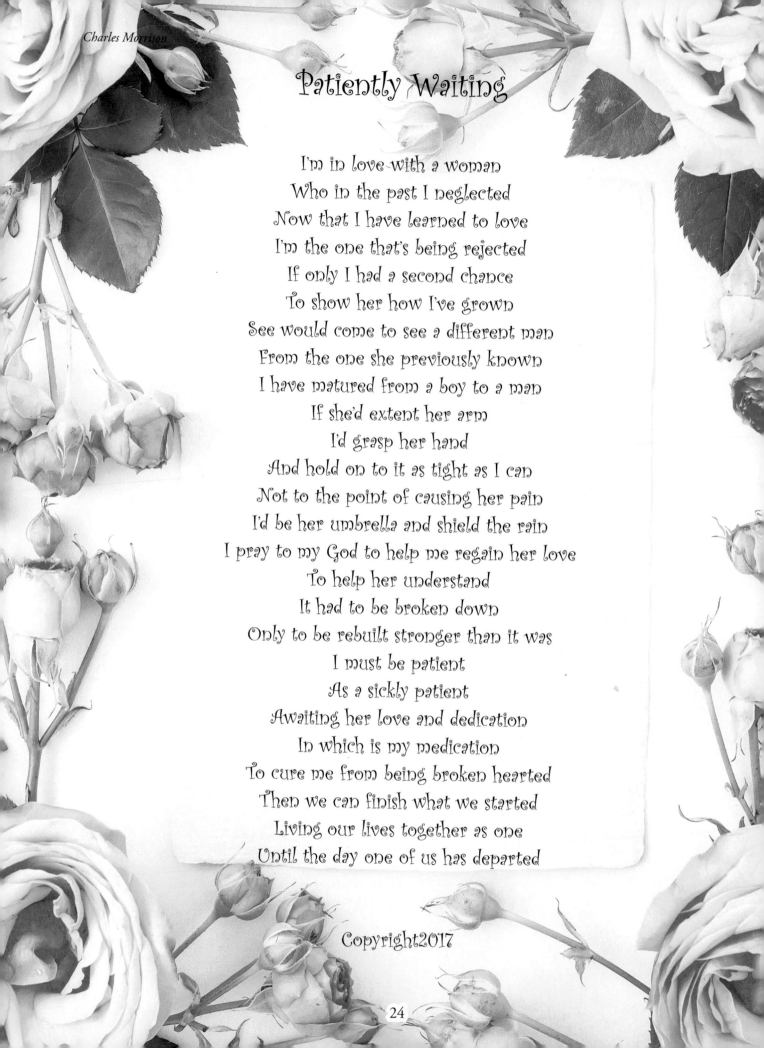

Charles Morrison

Patiently Waiting

I'm in love with a woman
Who in the past I neglected
Now that I have learned to love
I'm the one that's being rejected
If only I had a second chance
To show her how I've grown
See would come to see a different man
From the one she previously known
I have matured from a boy to a man
If she'd extent her arm
I'd grasp her hand
And hold on to it as tight as I can
Not to the point of causing her pain
I'd be her umbrella and shield the rain
I pray to my God to help me regain her love
To help her understand
It had to be broken down
Only to be rebuilt stronger than it was
I must be patient
As a sickly patient
Awaiting her love and dedication
In which is my medication
To cure me from being broken hearted
Then we can finish what we started
Living our lives together as one
Until the day one of us has departed

Copyright2017

Reduced time

What a world
What a world
What has this world become
When Gods judgment comes
He won't be judging a person
By the size of their income
It's by means of His wisdom
I've been able to see
No matter what it looks like
The best things in life are free
I'm reminded of this fact every time
One of my children smile up at me
So whatever our goals
As we scurry about in a haste
Remember all things are replaceable
Lost time is a real waste
We turn circle after circle
We look under and over
What we are looking for
Is right before our face
A little less time trying to earn
Is a little more time trying to learn
Time to teach, time to reach
Time to love
Time to give praise, honor and glory
To the one true God above
The time left is reduced

Copyright 2017

Charles Morrison

Blessed

Inside out I'm blessed by God to really see
Focused on the truth
I truly long to be
I have come a long way
But not yet fully complete
Being in, is the part of my life
I had to delete
It was big bucks
Lust of big butts
And big trucks
With big drugs in them
Every corner I turned
I had them spending
Darkness had me stuck in the game
Just spinning
While God looking down on me in shame
The devil grinning
I had to get out
I had to find a new way
I had to redirect my steps
So I could see another day
My days that good
I try to prove them to be good
I talk to some young people
And I'm misunderstood
It's like a whale in captivity
Telling a whale in the ocean
He needs to hope thru a Hula Hoop to eat
The ocean whale says
"Everything I need to live and exist is in the ocean
I eat for free"

THE CURE

"Let your kingdom (GOVERNMENT) come.
Let your will take place, as in heaven, also on earth."
Jesus Christ
(Son of God)

IT IS NOT SACRIFICE

IF YOU DO NOT FEEL IT

IF IT DOES NOT BRING YOU PAIN

IF YOU DO NOT SAY OUCH

IT IS NOT SACRIFICE

Charles Morrison

Rejoice

It's always sad at the death of a loved one
A daughter or son life gone at the sound of a gun
Took out in street violence
Or soldiers rejoicing of war being won
While their brothers and sisters are casualties
Sleep in deaths silence
Mothers and fathers reliance on drugs
Injecting needles in there arms contaminating their blood
Uncles, aunts, grandmas and granddads
Life taken away for material processions they had
Nephews and nieces perish slowly in hospitals
While their hope is little in vaccines for infectious diseases
So many needless calamites that pray on our families
And cut short the lives of our friends
That's why we need Gods Kingdom
To bring mans enemy death to an end
And free us from enslavement of our inherited sin
Resurrect the ones fallen
To a new system
So they can all start again
How loving is that
So yes
You will mourn and grieve the lost of your loved one
But have no fear
Rejoice in Gods Kingdom
It's a fact that it's near

Copyright 2017

Where Would I Be

Where would I be
Without Gods mercy, patience and love
His undeserved kindness
Would I be in the rut of this worlds
Dense dark blindness
Its timeless immorality
Fornication and lust
It embraces so causally
Its excessive drinking
Misguiding thinking
Its ill gotten gain
Would I be living like a king
Unjustly benefitting from the lowly ones pain
Would these seeds of Satan infiltrate my brain
Would these acts of ungodly deeds be my trade
If the sacrifice of His son He would not of made
If losing his favor I was not afraid
If I wasn't looking forward to being reunited
With my love ones in the grave
And I wasn't being fed the proper food
At the proper time from His slave
Then how would I behave
Without Gods mercy, patience and love
His undeserved kindness
Where would I be

Copyright2017

Charles Morrison

Gods Standards of Love

Love by mans standards or;
Love in Gods eyes
Love without fear of God
Is fueled by lust and lies
Hurt, pain and sorrow
With no trust in love tomorrow
All hope in love is lost
Bitterness and resentment becomes the result
But on the other hand
Love by Gods standards make room for love to expand
Makes room for love to grow
It makes for patience and understanding
So that the inner person you may come to know
By God standards love is long-suffering and kind
Love is not jealous; it does not get puffed up
It does not brag on things that it has
Love does not behave indecently
Or looks for its own interest
Love does not become provoked
Or keep account of injury
Love rejoices with the truth
Love bears all things
Believes, hope and endures all things
God's standard of love is written at 1 Corinthians chapter 13
Starting at verse 4 is where it dwells
By Gods standards
Love never fails

Provider of Escape

Every morning I awake
It's the same routine
I need an escape
I wish I had a cape
So I could fly far away
To a new scene
Somewhere serene
Where the load is light
Where my work is incorporated with my natural way of life
My natural existence
Where perfect people reside under perfect conditions
This was Gods purpose when He created the earth
The first man Adam neglected its worth
Today generation after next conditions become worse
I look to the hour for Gods anger to burst
For He is the source that truly provides escape
So for His day I patiently wait
For His Kingdom on earth I pray for it daily
This is way that God will save me
From my everyday routine
My secular work inside this system of things

Copyright 2017

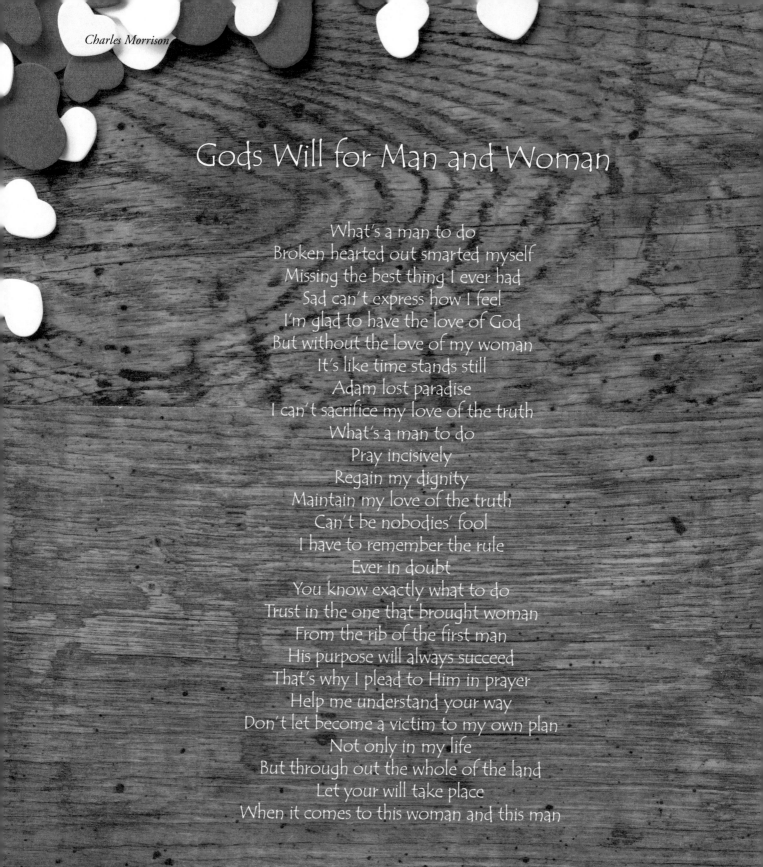

Charles Morrison

Gods Will for Man and Woman

What's a man to do
Broken hearted out smarted myself
Missing the best thing I ever had
Sad can't express how I feel
I'm glad to have the love of God
But without the love of my woman
It's like time stands still
Adam lost paradise
I can't sacrifice my love of the truth
What's a man to do
Pray incisively
Regain my dignity
Maintain my love of the truth
Can't be nobodies' fool
I have to remember the rule
Ever in doubt
You know exactly what to do
Trust in the one that brought woman
From the rib of the first man
His purpose will always succeed
That's why I plead to Him in prayer
Help me understand your way
Don't let become a victim to my own plan
Not only in my life
But through out the whole of the land
Let your will take place
When it comes to this woman and this man

Copyright 2017

Fear of God

Jesus is my Lord
He is King of Gods Kingdom
And our savior
I communicate in his name
to his Father in prayer
His prophecies are coming to pass
His Dads day is getting near
That's why
I can't be controlled by the
things of this world
Because Jehovah the only one
The only God that I fear

Copyright 2017

Free by Faith by Works

I'm surrounded by the enemy

The enemy has no face

I have to be like Daniel

Led by my faith

Backed up by my works

In the pit of the lions

I feel no hurt

I'm like a whale in the ocean

I'm free by Gods word

Not like the whales that hop thru hula hoops

Captive in Sea World

Copyright 2017

A Day in the Life

What's in a day
I awake
I pray
I see
I feel
I touch
I hear
I pray
I taste
I speak
I listen
I help
I hurt
I love
I pray
As I lay down to sleep
I have lived
Life is in a day

Copyright 2017

Dust to Dawn

Oh what has man become
In the image of
The son of destruction
Comfortable in our darken state
Full of greed, lust and hate
Taken to drugs as a way to escape
Then the drugs become a god in the way
A better day is what I look forward to
Gods' promises soon to be true
Extinction of this system for one that's new
Building houses with our own hands and living tax free
Eating from the cultivating of our own hands
The way God purposed it to be
You see today's economics will be no more
Replaced by spiritual things to help us grow
Spirituality helps us back to our natural sense
Peace of mind and spiritual bliss
Accurate knowledge and understanding of Him
And His son who love is near

A Message from the Most High

It's like no one knows
Know one sees
Some do not even care
Time is running out
We do not have left too many years
If we pray for Gods Kingdom
Here on earth
As in heaven
We have to be well prepared
It's like being down by two
With the bases loaded
This is the last period
Or the ninth inning the ending
People know what I'm saying
This is no game
This is our lives
Only the stupid will be playing
This message I'm just relating
With no delaying please get to praying
Repent with true sincere ness
God will give us His forgiveness
He only ask for faith
Backed up with the work
Of carrying out His business
Remember, this is not my message
I am just His witness

Copyright 2017

GODS KINGDOM

Gods Kingdom
The answer to mans problems
No earthly man or earthly government
Can solve them
Reality is that
Earthly man and earthly government
Are the problem
But by Gods Kingdom
Death, sickness, war and poverty will all be swallowed
Gods Kingdom on earth
As He intended it to be at Adams creation
A paradise filled and complete with perfect mankind
The lame one will dance
An a array of beautiful colors will be on display for the blind
Sweet praises to Jehovah
Deaf ears soon to hear
From the mouths of the mute
As they sing out with great cheer
Gods day Armageddon the wicked should fear
But the righteous rejoice and spread the good news
Gods Kingdom is near

Copyright 2017

Printed in the United States
By Bookmasters